Mandelson! Mandelson!
A Memoir

DAVID HERD lives and works in the public sector.

T0166912

DAVID HERD

Mandelson! Mandelson!

A Memoir

CARCANET

Acknowledgements

Thanks are due to the editors of the following magazines in which some of the poems in this book first appeared: *PN Review*, *The Enthusiast*.

First published in Great Britain in 2005 by
Carcanet Press Limited
Alliance House
Cross Street
Manchester M2 7AQ

A CIP catalogue record for this book is available from the British Library
ISBN 1 85754 818 3
The publisher acknowledges financial assistance from Arts Council England

Typeset in Monotype Ehrhardt by XL Publishing Services, Tiverton
Printed and bound in England by SRP Ltd, Exeter

O Captain! my captain! rise up and hear the bells;
Rise up – for you the flag is flung – for you the bugle trills,
For you bouquets and ribbon'd wreaths – for you the shores a-crowding
For you they call, the swaying mass, their eager faces turning.

Walt Whitman, 'O Captain! My Captain!',
from 'Memories of President Lincoln'

He is the final builder of the total building,
The final dreamer of the total dream,
Or will be.

Wallace Stevens, 'Sketch of the Ultimate Politician'

My project will be complete when the Labour Party
learns to love Peter Mandelson.

Tony Blair, 2 March 1996

Contents

Disclaimer

The question is, 'Are you happy?'

There are other questions of course, questions it would be equally useful to dwell on, questions such as 'How can I be good?', or 'What do I need to know?', 'What can I forget?' (names? dates?), 'How often does a person need to be told?'; 'Which way fate?', 'Is this really what you expected?', 'What more can I do to promote a just society?', 'Is more less?', 'I mean *really*, what you expected?', 'In what state, if there was such a thing, would I find my eternal soul?'

These are big questions; questions to which great minds have dedicated a lifetime's head-scratching, over which much tea has been slurped, and many a pair of shoulders hunched. Then there are others, smaller if in their own way no less pressing questions, questions such as, 'How hard should I work?', and 'Relative, say, to a butcher, how much money should I make?', and 'Who pays?', and then again, 'Who pays?', and 'If this is not what I expected, what did I expect?', and 'How do I measure up?', and 'In what circumstances is it appropriate to discriminate?', and 'What price frankness?', and 'When is it appropriate to make an offering?'. A particular favourite of mine is, 'Should I choose my words carefully?', or rather, 'Should I choose my words carefully, or with great care?', or 'Jesus, how much does a person really have to put up with?', and 'Who audits the auditors?', 'And then again, who pays?'. 'Trust: good or bad?' 'Sincerity: good or bad?' 'Weaselling out of things: how bad is that?' 'What, if anything, has poetry got to do with politics?' 'Should I choose my words carefully?' 'Do I deserve a big house?' 'What price frankness?' 'Does all that alters in fact persist?' 'Is it true that poetry never made anything happen?' It is true, of course, poetry never made anything happen. (Politicians at this point might want to turn to page 34.) 'How comfortable are you?' 'Do you feel relaxed in your universe?' 'Are there some days you feel more than a little hemmed in, like you can't quite breathe, as if there's no possibility of expansion?' 'Looking back at it now, is this what you'd been given to expect?' 'Do you fit the bill?' 'Does the bill fit you?' 'If you were drawing up the bill now, what would it look like?' 'Who pays?' 'How come some people pay more than others?' 'At what point in human history did it all go wrong?' 'If called upon to represent yourself, I mean really represent yourself, clothes and everything, what would you say?' 'Trust: good or bad?' 'Subtlety: good or bad?' 'Taking care: good? or bad?'

The trouble with questioning, of course, is that once you've started it's hard to stop ('Stopping: good or bad?', 'Being stopped?') But since one has to stop somewhere, and since only a madman would try to answer more than one question at time, it is best that for the moment we concentrate on the question we most owe it to ourselves to answer; the question, surely, we were put on God's earth to contemplate ('God: good or bad?') – 'What makes us happy?'

Sex is good. Or at least, good sex is good. Bad sex, it should be underlined, was never anything to write home about. Food also, although clearly here we enter the vexed arena of taste: chowder, say, or croûte de pâtés fricassées. Breathing – we should not, and especially in this dark time, forget breathing – the exchange of oxygen and carbon dioxide with the external world. Circulation generally. The right to remain silent. The willing and unrestricted exercise of limbs. (Pleasure: good or bad?) The historic season of ardour. An acquaintance with bodies not one's own. [By which of course, I mean physical bodies, bodies of land say, or water: funding bodies can go straight to hell.] Freedom (good or bad?). At any rate some degree of autonomy. A small corner of one's existence not given over to getting through. Time (good or bad?). Solidarity (good or bad?). Light entertainment? Moral rectitude? Acting on a whim. Not acting on another person's whim. Trust (good or bad?). Sincerity (good or bad?). 'What is to be done?' 'What even now might be undone?' Not watching on as one's whole system of government is reduced to a flicker of personality. And I don't know about you, but I think that would really cheer me up, put the spring back in my step, the proverbial cock back in my hoop. As in cock-a-hoop. As in, 'Today I'm cock-a-hoop.' Not being lied to – although of course you can't ask for everything. Except that you can, actually, ask for everything, that is. It's just that on the whole people don't. Communication: good or bad? Personality: good or bad? Having it all ways. Having stopped.

Not that anybody ever said it would be easy. Only the other day for instance, these and other issues on my mind – the timing of the tides, the strange disappearance of my passport, breakfast, whether, as some people insist, we get the politicians we deserve – I pushed my chair out, walked away from my desk. And breathing [oesophagus, lungs, alveoli], I nodded to a neighbour, who sort of nodded back, made my way to the high street, because all that persists does in fact alter, past the florist and the bank towards the new building. Which it has to be said is coming on nicely. There are to be a number of houses above a row of shops, a hall where on Mondays and Thursdays people will be able to learn Pilates, Tuesdays cookery, Fridays Ceroc; changing facilities; a meeting house; a forum for debate; a well resourced public library, featuring, in particular, extensive holdings in Greek and Roman thought – a first edition of Rabelais. [Whatever.]

BEGINNINGS

About These Parts

And friend, listen, it will soon be raining,
Though the wind might not blow and there is no famine
For night after night when the world is abed [asleep]
Trucks run freely toward the Norfolk coast.
To pick up what? People I suppose
Bound for Hackney and parts of Manchester I won't name
[I could name them but I won't name them]
Parts of Newcastle, parts of Leeds;
Rochester [*Christ*], parts of East Lancashire,
There are parts of Walsall I will never name
Not if you burn me – abed, asleep –
We welcome you, children, to these nameless parts.

And come, quick, because we too have starlings
Pleased – who wouldn't be – with their bronze-green plumage.
Voice: a harsh descending '*tcheeer*'.
Also a medley of clear whistles, clicks, rattles and chuckles
Woven into a long, rambling song.
And so you should make yourselves at home [or for God's sake try to],
We have blueberry muffins, a warm bed.
Starlings. I have a starling on my roof right now
                                        elaborating perfectly.
He's happy as Larry.
                        Is Larry happy?

My Young Youth

When I was young I had no secrets.
I would shit and piss and shriek and piss
So that frankly anybody who cared to inquire
Could know all there was to know about me.

I tell you, truly, it was an unholy state;
And I think, perhaps, the reticence
With which I now go out into the world
A consequence of the bad old days.

For instance, I have colleagues,
Good, sweet colleagues,
Unaware that on vacation
I am the assistant ambassador chief

To the young republic of Kazakhstan;
And friends, friends I have sung and danced with
Friends I have stepped to the brink and back with
In all the years we have known and wept

Have only met one of my wives.
For instance, a year ago this same morning
I walked out from an unfamiliar building
Along a street that was largely new to me

Lined with trees, to a strange square,
Where because it was early people were selling newspapers
From fold-away tables in fold-down hats
And in cafés women of all ages,

Some of them old enough to be the others' mothers,
Chatted on – about love maybe –
Banging out used-up coffee grounds.
A guy's tie blew up and all

About the place people looking
Like this was a good time for them
Walked to work, past shop windows, ambling
Into the primrose change;

That soon enough would sweep through this corner of the world
Neglecting nobody, stunning some
Into the functionally unavoidable thought
That adaptation is a beautiful demand;

That even now on the slopes of the Andes
A man waits for the first snow.
Pulse good. Breathing excitable.
I haven't told anyone that.

A Statement of Intent

These are long days.
Long enough to build a boat onto –
If it wasn't the boat yard had been parcelled out –
Or a house, roughly the size of your present one
Only with more windows this time, more light;
A shack, set back from the main cross-street
If subject materially to the prevailing winds
Battering in from the mid-Atlantic –
I have known wind could blow a grown man down;
A shack of a shack, ruin of a young man's ruin –
These are the thoughts of a young girl –
Nestled bravely above a medium-sized conurbation.
I have travelled widely among the Norfolk Broads.

All of which is why when the workmen come round
We sit and talk gently about the fabric of their
Lives – my life too, although that hardly comes
Into it – the perpetual journey towards self-fulfilment;
About reading and how in the early morning
All is possible in a made-up world.
And we tire of each other of course, which
Is why the work gets done –
And for the most part to our mutual satisfaction –
Gleaming, the height of a modest sepulchre.
And these too we will number among our achievements.

And these, too, on these long enough days
When so much is possible and so little gets done
Except talking a lot and sometimes listening
Raking over, mucking in.
And a house, built the way houses should always be built.
A man approaches from the beaten track.
'I come to you skilled in all forms of maintenance.'
'Sit down,' I tell him. 'We have much to talk about.'

In which the Poet, Trying to Come up with a Title for the Book he is Writing, becomes Anecdotal; and his Loyal Companion of Several Years' Standing Helps Out by Throwing a Log on the Fire

Juvenilia,
The Grand Gesture,
Blaze of Glory,
The Peter Mandelson Years,
The Voice of the Shuttle,
A Book at Bedtime,
Summer in Buenos Aires,
Poetry Please,
A Question of Upbringing,
Hymns Ancient and Modern,
Diary of a Nobody,
AOL,
Argosy,
The Last Mutual,
The Honest Dealer,
Destiny's Child,
The Why of the Wind,
('We stand as nowhere')
England, England,
The Peter Mandelson Years,
A Seemly World,
An Exile's Letter,
A Lover's Complaint,
A Lonely Girl,
A Guide to the Trees of Britain
and Mainland Europe,
A Network of Asters,
On Brighton Beach,
The London Years,
On Dartford Crossing,
Provide Provide,
On Battersea Bridge,
A Fistful of Dollars,
A Roomful of Mollahs,
A Mouthful of Scholars,
On General Release,

A Heartful of Dolours,
Collage with Colours,
Aubade in Silver, Blue and Green,
The Singles Collection,
The Modular Option,
Captain Correlli's Mandolin,
Naive and Sentimental Music,
My Captain, My Captain,
The Peter Mandelson Years,
Sun Rising in the Absence of Trees,
I Alone Escaped to Tell Thee,
My Spirit so High it was all over the Heavens,
Southend, at Dead of Night,
My Spirit so High I nearly Crashed the Car,
On the Road,
On the Buses,
Dial 4 to Change your Personal Options,
We Campaign in Poetry, Govern in Prose,
The Auditors,
Many are the Fin-backs,
To have been so Happy is a Kind of Promise,
As When a Child I Sat on the Stoop,
And spoke the State Licenses,
A Kind of Blue,
A Kind of Loving,
And if it isn't Kept that doesn't Matter,
If only the Argumentation could be Conducted Openly Enough,
Your Old Men Shall Dream Dreams,
Lift up your Eyes and Look on the Fields
A Silver Rolls Royce on Fifth Avenue,
(Which I only mention
Because I actually saw it
From the steps of the New York Public Library
On a warm afternoon full of promise,
People skating, traffic stopped,
Going about each other's business
Like someone just coined the phrase
'Not a care in the world',
And the task that day
Was to try to describe it,
Which was a delusion, I know,
But I didn't think so,
As I sat on the steps,

Don't want to think so),
Dissidence,
Orphan Thoughts,
Juvenilia,
The Grand Gesture,
Mandelson! Mandelson!
Projective Verse,
Would you please throw another
Log on the fire.

Notes Towards a New Method of Institutional Audit

Petals on a wet, black bough.

IN WHICH THE POET GOES TO WORK, AND GOES TO
LONDON [UNNOTICED], AND ON ONE OCCASION HIS
WIFE COMES BACK

Cherries

So. I have been wondering lately,
When I haven't been wondering about other things –
The guttering, for instance, I worry so much about the guttering –
I have been wondering lately how you present a poem
To people who don't like poems.

For instance, the other day I was in a part of London
I know well and which I shall assume
You know well also – narrow streets,
Blue-fronted, aspirational shops –
Where I was buying coffee, coffee from Honduras
[Do you worry also about aspirational economics?]
And it was early – what passes anyway for early in London –
And so the shops were half open, half awake
And people who looked like they had nothing better to do
Were walking out as if they lived here,
Like they had friends who thought they *ought* to live here,
But for circumstance [though they were not wretched].
And one of them, one of the especially pretty ones,
Was sitting on steps, her back to a statue
Which had writing on it, and she was wearing sandals.
Not wretched either. It was a warm day.

And so we said hello, and I bought my coffee,
And then I turned a corner, and then another corner,
Thinking really of nothing in particular –
Alastair Campbell, maybe, his early career,
How he carps on, how other people carp back at him,
Cherries, how richly they deserve their name:
CHERRIES, how I ate one recently and if I had ever known it
I remembered how sweetly in earnest they could be,
How one afternoon I walked in on a Whistler,

    'We crash on blithely. It is NOT the same.'

And? And?

    'We crash on blithely.'

I have to my right a small suitcase,
Which my wife bought and which she no longer uses.
I am thinking of keeping my poems in it.

Modern Love

It's six o'clock and I'm sitting here
Drinking coffee and thinking of you.
Clouds black against a blue background,
Telling me somewhere
The sun is up,
Build comprehensively –
And the birch,
I notice,
Skinny against the chimney
Taller than it should be
Could use some leaves.
I leave the room
Make some more coffee
('You drink too much coffee')
Come back to my desk.
Clouds black against the thinnest branches
Property of starlings
Thinning branches
And your listening
Because I know you will be listening –
In the shadow of a raspberry bush –
How Peter's quit.

I breathe.
Breathe again.
A wind picks up
And the branches catch it
Property of starlings
Falling back.
Pipes knock about the place.
Like someone took a hammer to cathedral railings
Heralding the morning.
Knocking stops.
And a noise that I can't name,
Because it doesn't need naming,
Traffic maybe,
Lorries,
Trucks,
Moving freight from its regional centres,
Heralding morning,

Takes the frequency down.
I set my cup –
Blue –
Beside my telephone –
Touchtone –
And now I'm thinking of you thinking
And I see his face.

I guess
I'm guessing now
I can only guess –
But truly, I guess,
There must have been a moment –
Stars fading in the western sky
Not a branch without blossom
That could bear blossom
[Crowds from the precincts of the capital coming
From their trains and their buses people coming]
A moment,
Surely,
Besides the river
(Isn't it time for the birds to sing?)
When to utter
A syllable
'Kiss' for instance
'Kiss' to camera
(Western sky)
In the crowd
Say –
'Bliss'
For instance –
When simply to utter a syllable altered …

I reach for my cup
Sip my coffee.
Watch the branches play
Barely against the chimney,
Pitching forward,
Falling back,
Recalling thinking,
The day you told me –
Getting the balance
Of optimism right –

'We are not alone in the world,
But we might as well be' –
That, actually,
It is possible to plan,
Only like in a film
In which nothing happens –
Leaves landing on a forest floor –
There are days,
Months even,
When you have to stop –
Forgetting everything
That doesn't
Help –
And just turn the cards over,
Jack,
Seven,
Repeating the action,
[Seven, Jack]
Until you've forgotten,
Totally forgotten
That you're sitting in a carpark,
That you're on a wall,
Sitting, with the themes
Of your conversation:

'Not alone in the world,
But might as well be.'
You stand up.
We stand up.

Not alone, but might as well be.

Pitching forward.
Falling back.

Note: Peter quit twice, the first time on December 11 2001, after money was borrowed and he bought a big house: 'Through my misjudgement I've allowed the impression to be created of wrongdoing.' ☺

Mass Observation

Two women on a university campus.
One with her head upon the other's shoulder;
The other with her arm around the other's neck.

On Once Seeing Gary Hume's 'Daffodils' in Hoxton (I Wanted to Whistle)

1

See: how they conduct themselves,
  These bright young people;
  How they make themselves
  Apparent!

Boy meets girl: at a café of their choosing
              after the working day is done

Optimal.
                    Hey! Hey!

She orders. He has what she has.

(One step forward.
One step back.
One step forward.
One steps back.)

Ahem!

When the others arrive. Acknowledging the others!
This is hardly to be thought an inconvenience.

Then the wind blows serene against the buildings.

A couple leave
            object intact.

2

Further to the east spaces widen. Processes
blend, press apart, as the millionth
encounter on the avenue today

passes off without impact. A car starts.
Sundry women come and go. Traffic
yellows to the angle of evening
and a heavy man leans against a window.

– Hey heavy man, heavy man, haven't you had enough!
[This is the voice of the precinct's children.]
And the shutters roll up. *One step forward.*
And the stars come out. [Regardless.]

3

Even so, he loved the City!

Late at night [when only a few were still working]
He would run about from street to street
Pointing directly at the highest buildings.

'Look! he would say, 'Look! Here is the Bank of Bolivia!
And here, look, taller! The People's Bank of Shanghai!
Here are Finland! Brazil! Turkey! Ottawa!

Here are banks of The Yemen, Sweden, Spain.

And here is the moon, climbing lightly.
It is a clear night. There are only a few clouds.

Plainly.
                [Someone should carry them home.]

A man steps forward
                                whistling.

To E.P. – Connoisseur, Modern

These are my terms.

I grant you the value of true pastiche –

If you grant me the virtù of pastee.

Almonds

It's almonds outside and in the city
The moon like a golf ball sits
On a tower like an egg. The wheel glitters.
It's January and I'm wearing shirt sleeves!

Your conversation brightens.
How men building work under lights
And how passengers slip away gladly.
You tell me your plans. I tell you mine.

The beauty, we agree, is in the framework;
The supporting thought. How the dense grace
Of the Brooklyn Bridge must once
Have performed the same function. Only brassier.

'Apples of gold and silver,' I said.
Lemons and limes more like.
A woman on the bridge is cajoled
Into leaving. Everywhere shines.

Apples

You call from the train. I come.
On the platform a man with a tenancy agreement
Stamps wine from his boots. Like a dog.
Good boots. Boots a man could be pleased with. It is 5.14. The world
reddens.

In the street they quicken, and so soon
A group of refugees in ochre and orange
Chat and smoke in their own language.
Wisteria brushes a corrugated wall. Like normal.

In the shops and the churches the talk
Is of winter, and so I dream of coats –
How once in Moravia you brought an apple-red trench coat.
Nothing you or I had packed was equal.

And so wives kiss husbands and in flamingo pinks
Conversations branch and continue. I take your bag
And it's like nothing intervenes. Like laughing
The boys know the schedule.

March 9th, 2001

'I did not lie, I did not deceive, I did not set out to mislead.'

[Whatever]

IN WHICH THE POET SPEAKS OF TIME SPENT

IN AMERICA, WHILE NOTING, IN PASSING,

AN ALIMENTARY COMPLAINT

In Which the Poet Speaks of Time Spent in America, While Noting, in Passing, an Alimentary Complaint

For four months I lived in America.
It was the happiest time of my life.
The ocean, the elections, the human attainments!
That time we ate bagels
                     on the corner of 40th street and 7th Avenue
And only the man who sold the *New York Times* –
And he couldn't have cared less
                     because the sun was shining
On store-owners mid-town –
Knew we were there.

I tell you it was totally Emily Dickinson
And had it been bagel
                 was my snack of choice
(If I didn't bloat
                wasn't slightly gluten intolerant)
I think that day on Manhattan Island
I might have been as a soul set free
Screening calls, dissolving projects,
Watching as planes made their appearance
Not watching as aeroplanes
                   circled back.

And not for the first time.

Once, in Europe, I spent the morning in a slatted chair
reading a book – this would have been some time in the early 90s –
peopled with change and the desire for change and every so
often I'd get up, make some coffee, go back to my book:
because I could obviously – the physical effort was negligible –
but happy also I was on a hill; with the whole arrangement,
the way the sea started and ended, giving out upon a quiet beach
parked with boats, the size of boats mostly, sails shaped
the size of lilac sails.

Another time, not quite so fabled I grant you [*although the allocation
was not less sweet*] I left a building expecting rain – hours the city
had been dogged by rain, all the talk was of how much rain –
and I stepped outside and found the rain had stopped. And which

in itself might not have proved sufficient, expect that morning
I had woken up, from an adequate sleep, quite largely rested
to the sound of a woman preparing food; or preparing something,
and if not singing exactly, not not establishing a strong theme,
from Strauss perhaps: *Ariadne auf Naxos*. Aware, apparently,
that the light had changed.

Completely.

But then not of course completely also.
It was food.
It probably wasn't Strauss.
More settled somehow.
Not quite so keen to be splendid.
The way sometimes we say snow 'settles' on windows.
And sometimes doesn't.
Except it wasn't snow.

America, though, that's something else isn't it.
(I mean the landmass, clearly, and not the state.
Not that that there's not an overlap;
Just something over also.
Let's call it 'space' for a moment.
Let's call it 'light and space'.)
Call it, 'standing, beside a body of water',
Trees growing towards the water's edge,
And there is State, this is Maine or Massachusetts,
But there is standing also, in unseasonable clothes,
If happily. To clarify, 'My clothing though unseasonable
was happy'; 'I was happy standing in seasonably inappropriate
clothes'; 'Regardless, I was standing, happy in Massachusetts.'
Or Maine.
Yes, come to think of it, it could have been Maine.
In jeans and a T-shirt I had picked up in New York.
The T-shirt that is.
The jeans we bought elsewhere.
England arguably.
                              'In cool light.'

Exile's Letter

Dear Uncle Maurie,
This morning I remembered that day we took a boat out
        to the island.
How the creek was calm as we waded to the beach
And the butterflies made even the bulwarks yellow.
You stood on a wall and told the story of the place;
        its topography:
How the hills to the north of the outlet were a recent
        addition.
You showed me the ruin, and as rain threatened
I don't know how many hills we must have crossed
        together.
But we rowed back, I remember, to a sulphurous blue;
With the lights coming on in the warehouse:
You singing to the sound of your stroke –
Me, with my head in your lap.

It is months, now, since I arrived in this country.
And all I have met with is kindness.
Many commodities are in good supply – coffee, sugar,
        raisins –
And each day in my building, as I empty my waste,
Somebody tells me I must come and go as I please:
Which I confess I am prone to, especially at dawn,
And what with the activity and the events in the square
The world never seemed so gently disposed
        toward the seasons.
First it was summer; then spring:
And now the cherry blossom is crushing against my
        window.
I tell you Uncle, the colour, I wish I could show you.
How it fastens the city. Breaks my heart.

I can walk to work, if I leave early,
Following the river till it begins to widen, and crossing at the moment
        it rises,
And where later people who don't know the city
Stand and look out on its various districts, assemble parts.
And I have space enough,
        to heap my belongings,

But progress is slow, time short,
And though I am sure we will soon be approaching completion,
Yesterday afternoon, as I drafted my findings, I lifted my cup
        to see geese arrive.
And I thought of you, in those trousers of yours
Gone in the hip with your soles remade,
Your shambling coat in that distant parish
Bellowing out because no-one could hear
'England, I quit! I have fallen in love with another.'
And how your laughter confused me, and now I am here
And the rumour has circled there are few now who speak
        of advancement.

So I could go north, which would mean more travelling –
Though fewer commitments, and as the leaves thicken, aigrettes lifting
        from the valley floor.
The plumage, they tell me, is treasured in decorative cultures.
I have names and addresses.
                    We should speak soon.

Mass Observation

The best omelette I ever ate
                          was in Marblehead.

Prudence

It is morning and so the sun falls upon the veranda,
Across the chequered print of the yellowing table cloth, on to the stone
      surround.
Deck chairs, into which a heavy man might slump, built of hard dark
      wood, slung low to the ground, catch the light; deposit patterns
      on a neutral background; verticals and curves upon a white-
      washed wall.
From her window a woman looks out towards her husband, across the
      medium of morning, to an outsize sun.

Around the corner [which is where he is headed] some men are working.
They are building a house, and the contractor, who is eager for his
      family to settle, lease the apartment he has roomed above his
      own, visits often.
This makes the men jump! And as no one will be happy until the last nail
      is nailed, the interior complete,
One man, stripped to the waist, tattoos depicting life at sea,
Throws bricks – two at a time – to another man standing on the scaffold.
Often, as the bricks reach the top of their trajectory, they part and this
      would be impossible to handle,
If the man receiving, leaning from the scaffold, his bulk dependent, on
      load-bearing bars
Didn't catch them at the moment of downward momentum, as the weight
      shifts.
There, he dropped one.

And here! a block away, and for only ten dollars, a Russian woman will
      wash, dry and fold your laundry.
She will also deliver, within the neighbourhood, and within the
      neighbourhood this gives her the edge.
Even so, on weekdays throughout August, the sun hot on the laundry
      step, the men from the grocery store opposite talking, peeling
      apples, she prefers you wait.
'Now,' she will tell you, 'I am very happy in Brooklyn.
To come here I had to cross many lines of latitude, leaving several of my
      family, far behind.
And when I arrived I didn't understand the graffiti: its inflated lettering,
      a new alphabet to me.
But now on Sundays, when my husband minds the shop and I'm making
      my way back from the city, sometimes if I crane I catch a love-lit

glance, from the tops of the buildings, and I thrill a little,
And I think of that summer, when I was home, and I took the train from
   Paveletsky station, and I was a girl then, and the summers were
   long, and we went to the Steppe.
What else is there?'

September 11th, 2001

Worked in the morning.

Watched TV.

IN WHICH PETER SPEAKS, AN EXTRAORDINARY RITUAL

TAKES PLACE, AND SOMEBODY,

SOMEWHERE, TAKES A DEEP BREATH

Peter's Poem

Happiness, of course, is all that counts –
Sweet bird, if only he would sing to me –
But life is complex, always pressure mounts;

And so, while I have known love, truly *would* pronounce
The equal to this, our careworn jamboree –
Happiness of course is all that counts.

It's like in the city sometimes, you're with friends, go to announce
How glad you are, how just then, when the world seemed to pause
                                                    momentarily –
But life is complex, always pressure mounts

So I move on, slightly sad a chance
Has passed, but there will be others, times to proclaim loudly:
HAPPINESS OF COURSE IS ALL THAT COUNTS

The words are big in my head already and I see the crowd bounce
A little as it leaves the hall, chuckling freely.
But life is complex, always pressure mounts.

So I hum quietly to myself, myself able to renounce,
And then myself renounced announce convincingly:
Happiness, of course, is all that counts;
But life is complex [*say* it!] pressure mounts.

Peter! Peter!

A Noh Play

The Noh plays are ancient one-act plays of Japan. The audience once dressed for them as for a religious service in elaborate ceremonial robes. The interest is in suggested action or tensions, and in the lyrics, dances and formalized gestures. The decor is symbolical. The musicians – traditionally three dancers, and a flute – appeared on stage. The actors stamped their feet at the conclusion of their speeches. The movement is photographic rather than dramatic. The audience is supposed to know all the plays by heart.

THE PERSONS

Voice 1 – will tend, on the whole, to be grumpy
Voice 2 – is something of a flash in the pan

The voices alternate. There *is* only one act.

SCENE: The open road. At one end of which, beneath a small mountain, a dwelling welcomes the disconsolate eye; at the other a pond, still, murky, stands in the shade of a great oak. Mountain, pond, oak, dwelling: all are painted in uprights to the side of the stage. A lay-by stands equidistant between them: the distances marked out clearly on the stage floor. Two men, *Voice (V)1* and *Voice (V)2* arrive grateful, exhausted, at said lay-by. They have been walking all night. The sun rises. Something heavy is on their minds.

Peter. [For some hours now *V1* has been silent. He is wearing a yellow and orange cloak. He raises his arms, as if himself sun-like. His speech is to be uttered in a tonally neutral voice.]

Peter. [Nodding – *V2* until now also silent – in recognition; his cloak is mauve.]

[They sit; each knowing there will be much more walking. It is not clear to the audience why they have stopped. They stand up. They sit down again. Each is emphatically not comfortable.]

Peter. [In this case the stress should be distributed evenly; each syllable stretched beyond its normal extent. One might think of a hyphen, Pe-ter; there is also discernible shift in tone: not cross exactly, quietly exasperated, towards tetchy. He stands up. Only as he stands up, as he tries to stand up, his leg becomes caught in the fold of his cloak. (Left *or* right; the actor may choose here; whichever tends best towards a graphic effect.)]

[Because what ensues is the play's single most dramatic moment. *V1* after much tugging and wrestling – the audience should be thinking here of Harold Lloyd, in an early masterpiece like *Good Cop, Fat Cop* – finally manages to haul himself up. Except that in hauling – and what should be emphasised here is effort, cartoon gestures signalling frustration and sweat – he has pushed his right (the actor's left is acceptable) through and into the hem of his coat. So that while he *is* up, he is only partially upright; the cloak is shin-length, so as it tightens, he stoops; and he is hopping, a picture of unaccountable fury, trying to work his entangled foot loose. Except that in working he kicks, pushing his foot further into the hem, and with each time he kicks, so the hood of his cloak is pulled down, and as he kicks he hops, so now is kicking *and* hopping; the unavoidable comparison is with a demented hen. And this – kick, hop, head lurching involuntarily; the image of a body uselessly at war with itself – goes on for minutes, to many it seems like hours; to some it seems like the rest of their life. Except that of course *V1*, having arrived exhausted, cannot sustain this expression of purposeless rage, so he collapses, breathless, beside his companion, his voice breaking into a barely audible wail.]

Peeeeeeeeterrrrrrrrrrr [The wail, haunting, weirdly entrancing – the audience by this time is on the edge of its seat – drifts preternaturally across the landscape; one is reminded inescapably of Tennyson's Maud. And on it goes, barely altering in intensity – an expression, eventually of pure duration, except that as such it become clear the sound must necessarily be taped, only the break is seamless, so one minute the actor is sounding, the next spectacularly voiceless, mute. Gapes. The effect is of noise through silence; the mouth's silence outlined by the continuous noise, shaped, attributed definition, until to everybody present the differential is clear. Whereupon, and here the judgement is technical, although in practice the moment is always the same, the pitch drops, steeply, disarmingly; the engineered voice becomes a clarinet. And sings, briefly, the allusion is to America, to Aaron Copland after World War Two, but the phrase is muffled, becomes Lutoslawski, becomes Anton Webern, becomes Thomas Adès.

Then nothing.

And for a while the sound is only of breathing ... until *V2*, elaborately, starts shaking his head ...]

Peter. [... he mumbles, the tone is of resignation.]

49

Peter. [*V1* also, now, is shaking his head.]

Peter. [Jointly, by way of announcement.]

Peter. [Sweetly, as if lying in bed.]

Peter. ['Your Mammy is coming to get you.']

Peter. [Laughing.]

Peter. [Laughs.]

Peter. [Now they are laughing totally.]

Peter. [Laughing. The audience laughs.]

Peter. [Fuck it. Laughing. Totally.]

Peter. [Fuck it. Totally. Stops.]

[And as the lights go down so the lights go up again. *V1* and *V2* have left the stage. The audience rises, not sure what it has witnessed – how long it has been here. There is stamping feet.]

How to Breathe

Single cell organisms can exchange oxygen and carbon dioxide directly with the external environment (the world), but this is obviously impossible for most cells of a complex organism like the human body; most cells of a complex organism like the human body being tucked away, discreetly, from sight. In order to survive, large animals (the elephant would be an example of a large animal) have had to develop specialised systems for the supply of oxygen and the elimination of carbon dioxide. These systems are not the same in all complex animals – in the case of the elephant what we're clearly talking about here is the trunk – since evolution often follows several pathways simultaneously. We call these pathways bio-diversity. [Excellent.] The organs of gas exchange with the external environment (the world) in fish are gills; those in man are lungs.

In a man or woman at rest, the body's cells consume approximately 200ml of oxgen per minute. This is a lot. Under conditions of severe oxygen requirement – like when you're exercising, for instance, or making love, fitting silently in a darkened room – the rate of oxygen consumption may increase as much as thirtyfold. Equivalent amounts of carbon dioxide are simultaneously eliminated. It is obvious, therefore, that mechanisms must exist which co-ordinate breathing with metabolic demands. We can call this mechanism the respiratory system.

The term respiratory system refers only to those structures which are involved in the exchange of gases between the blood and the external environment (the world). Oxygen has to be absorbed into the blood because the body depends on it. Carbon dioxide has to go out into the world because, frankly, there is nowhere else for it to go. The respiratory system comprises the lungs, the series of passageways leading to the lungs, and the chest structures responsible for movement of air in and out of the lungs.

[You might, at this point, like to think about your own breathing for a moment. Is it steady? Can you rely on it? Are your chest structures as responsible as they might be? Are your passageways clear? Are your lungs capacious? Do you exchange successfully with the world?]

We press on.

In order for air to reach the lungs, it must first pass through a series of air passages connecting the lungs to the mouth. There are two lungs, the right and the left, each divided into several lobes. Together with the heart, great vessels, oesophagus, and certain nerves, the lungs completely fill the chest (thoracic) cavity. Nor are the lungs simply hollow balloons – the hollow balloon is the wrong analogy – but have themselves a highly organised structure: air-containing tubes, blood vessels, elastic connective tissue. The air passages within the lungs are the continuation of those which connect the lungs to the nose and the mouth. This is where the world comes in. Together we will call these tubes the conducting tubes of the respiratory system. These tubes branch, and as they branch so they become smaller, and as they branch so they become more numerous; more numerous, even, than it is comfortable to imagine, the very smallest ending in tiny blind sacs. And it is here, in these tiny, sightless arenas that the exchange of gases actually occurs. We call these sacs the alveoli. Everything tends towards the alveoli.

Air.
Air can.
Air can enter.
Air can enter the respiratory passages either by the nose or mouth. The nose is good if you are eating, and is, anyway, the more conventional route. It [the air] then passes into the pharynx (throat), a passage common to the routes followed by air and food. The pharynx branches – *the pharynx branches!* – into two tubes: one (the oesophagus) through which food passes into the stomach, and one through which air passes into the lungs. We won't now here follow the food into the stomach, but will, with the air, press on down into the lungs. Down: the first portion of the air passage, called the larynx, houses the vocal cords; those two strong bands of elastic tissue, which stretch across the lumen of the larynx; strong enough, anyway, to prevent the lungs filling with food. The movement past them of air causes them to vibrate, initiating the many different sounds which constitute speech. For instance, 'Lumen', 'Larynx', 'Lungs', 'Oesophagus', 'Heart', 'Nerves', 'Alveoli'.

To conclude, breathing consists of an exchange of air between the atmosphere (the world) and the alveoli. This process includes the movement of air in and out of the lungs and the distribution of air within the lungs. Not only must a large volume of new air be delivered constantly to the alveoli (those unseeing sacs, sightless sites of exchange) but it must be distributed evenly to the millions of alveoli within each lung. Each single alveoli filling with each inspiration. We call this process ventilation.

There is more to breathing, more one could dwell on: the exchange of oxygen and carbon dioxide between air and lung capillaries by diffusion; the transportation of oxygen and carbon dioxide by the blood; the exchange of oxygen and carbon dioxide between the blood and tissues of the blood by diffusion as blood flows through tissue capillaries. Imagine it, though, millions of alveoli, simultaneously filling up.

In. Out.

      In. Out.

            We call this process ventilation.

Tuesday

Called Jack. Jack sounded edgy. He said to put all my money into government bonds pronto because the whole fairground was about to hit the tracks. Belly up. I listened. Jack was a good talker. But some days it wasn't good to talk to Jack. I put the phone down. Jack was still talking. Jack was always talking. It had been a long day. What with the news from home, and now Jack's metaphor. I tried to remember when I had last slept.

Slumbered. I thought. But for some reason my thinking was in decades only. The 1970s. That couldn't be right. And now I was tired. Maybe if I lay down for a moment. I lay down. On white linen. Sweetly aware that of all the hotels I had ever stayed in, these were probably the heaviest, best pressed sheets. If stiff. Someone knew hospital corners. I smiled as it dawned. The deathbed fold.

I was woken by the sound of a small French petrol engine abruptly occupying the public square, a display of shallow, alluvial sunlight; strangely certain where my money should be. I dressed, if largely involuntarily. Within minutes I was walking down the central street, which was wider, somehow more prone than I'd realised; locomotive, like there was sufficient space. Which is to say *was* [my emphasis]. Which is to say *is* only in the past tense. Which is to say I walked, prone, wider, in alluvial sunlight, along the central street. Past trees. Seagulls flocked ceaselessly. A woman shopped, from a comprehensive list, plumpish, visibly in her element, carrying on as if she carried on routinely, about the way things had changed recently, about the way things changed. Chatting, on, as the sun loped westward [*sloped*]; on, as a new set of particulars became clear. Drawing gratefully on a friend's cigarette. 'Mr. Fredericks, it's September.' *September.* 'It's here.'

My Life

The Story:

I was a fat child.
My wicked stepmother
force-fed me chicken sticks
so by the time I was seven
it took eight grown men
to lift me from
out of my ivory
bed.

Now I am old. I eat
little. I exercise daily
from dawn until dusk
and not till the goblin
tells me I'm done
do I settle my head
on my wooden
block.

The Lesson:

So my friends you
should learn that
the things of this
world are as nothing
compared to a virtuous
thought. I live on
water and air and
extract of corn; though
on occasion the goblin
will cook up a
knish.

The Poet's Dream

When I first met my wife –
I should say, rather, the woman who was to become my wife,
So as to avoid the impression
She was my wife before we met –
We fell in love,
Then we fell into bed
(Though I am hazy, I confess, as to the precise sequence).
We fell out occasionally,
Not of the bed you understand
(Actually this did happen,
One hilarious evening,
But some things are best kept
Between a man
And his wife);
Mostly, however, we fell about laughing,
So one night in the city,
As the sun hit the river,
I fell to my knees,
And thus we were wed.
Hereafter events took a precipitous turn –
My wife fell pregnant,
I fell into a job.
And you could say my daughter
Fell into the world.
I held her up for a moment.
It was so beautiful.

I have this dream sometimes that I'm Harold Lloyd, the silent American movie star. In the dream I am running away from a fat man, who turns out to be my boss, because in his restaurant, a moment earlier, I tripped while carrying this huge pile of plates. What followed, naturally, was unspeakable chaos – a lobster lands on rich lady's head – so now I'm being chased by my boss, a cop with a whistle, and unaccountably a large crowd of people who have emerged from nowhere onto the main street. Which is ok, because in a nearby airfield, a bi-plane is humming, primed for take-off; so I jump in, release the handbrake – having never driven a plane before much of what follows is conjecture – and seconds later I'm sailing over suburban America, Milwaukee I reckon, and life is sweet. At which point – and here there are

two things you have to remember: first that movies were shorter in those
days, second that Harold performed all his own stunts – the engine cuts out.
Dead. Nothing. One minute purring, like an over-fed baby. The next
it's August
and I'm standing on a mountain
and the plane has entered
a graceful dive.
And I'm aware that to somebody watching beneath me, my arc is a gesture
of radical will, only I can't find the catch, the ice is melting, and with little
choice but to work my self free,
I walk out
along the wing
step away
from a falling plane
acutely conscious, that at this juncture only the relative density of housing,
and the benign teleology of Hollywood's plots...
I hit a roof
which slows my descent somewhat, but I guess because the wood is brittle –
happily this is a clapboard house – I don't halt, but crash on through, into a
bedroom where a couple is asleep, each curved into the other's body, a man
and woman, husband, wife. And the curious thing is, this continues to
happen, I hit a floor,
and the ceiling gives way,
I hit a floor
and the ceiling collapses,
and the ceiling collapses,
say, after me

In Which the Poet and his Wife Address the State of the Nation

So we agreed:
that woman on the high street
her sari was more orange than peach.
You thought amber, maybe.
But I thought, if anything russet was closer.
Orange it was.
We moved on.

Later on the beach we had a debate,
On the state of the nation;
Or to be more precise the nation state –
Which one of us, I forget who,
Had heard was under threat.
Looking back I can't remember the details:
only that opposite us a woman
was sketching those cottages that are so
characteristic of this place;
and that behind it all the sea lapped
– slapped you said –
against the shore.
I remember thinking that this was the life.
'Not ours,' you said, correctly.

In the evening we listened eagerly
as a friend recalled her honeymoon.
France, Italy, then from Bari to Greece,
Albania, Macedonia, Paxos.
She had had, she said, the time of her life.
You begged to differ.
And I remember thinking that you might have been right,
But it was late,
And your meaning escaped me.

Untitled

I had this plan.
I would finish my book,
Greet my baby,
Make a start on another book.

So much for plans.
Who needs books anyway?
I will say goodnight now.
Sleep well.

IN WHICH THE POET CHECKS HIS BALANCE

On First Listening to Mahler's Second Symphony, otherwise known as the 'Resurrection'

Wheeeeee! Chickpeas glitter across the Bay of Naples,
And as if the soufflé wasn't enough
A swallow dives into a swallow dive,
Dives again, only this time with less feeling.
Dives the second time because the first time wasn't perfect –
Imagine the singer who hears his own applause,
Now imagine the singer who hears only singing
Who sings in singing of the intricacies of song,
And not – because here there is nothing intricate,
Nothing to which soul cannot allocate place;
A place, nothing to which soul cannot allocate
A place; or maybe nothing; or maybe nothing less
Than trumpets [points] gently augmented by oboes
'There is no punishment and no reward'
And no story, only a cor anglais
'Distorted, crazy'; 'all *is* quiet'.

A Builder Sings

Enough! A fat woman sat on the step, crushed
By the hand-me-down beauty of alpines.
The sea babbled. There are versions of the sea.
Summers it was buzzing, cokey.

More! A tubercular man, bent double,
Sucked up sweetpeas for the last time.
A rift opened – between a builder and his wife.
Singing, they sang, 'Forgive me!'

And, 'Believe me, because it is always like this!'
Storms rumbled purple across the plain.
Purple storms rumbled across the plain
Battering telegraph poles, people.

Because some days, days after it has rained,
The sea resembles a curate's egg.
Imagine it though, consenting to become the earth.
'Sometimes does.'
                                        Doesn't.

January 20th, 2003

Checked balance.

Two hundred and forty seven pounds
and sixty eight pence

credit.

In Person

I am three stories up
And here in the hayloft
It matters little what I say to you.
Matters less what you say to me –
Except where news of the neighbours is concerned.

And not that I have any – news that is.
The neighbours are well, they asked me to say so.
                                        In person.
They asked me to say so in person.
We agreed tomorrow.
Tomorrow should be fine.

Note to Self

Must make
provision for the future.

Must save
towards later, in life.

Shops and Houses

Hair like sand the old man removed to his hut
Beaten like cabinets left for the weather to play with
As a people sometimes will turn from the old monolith
Heavy from decades of hemming and hawing but
Grinning regardless and without emphasis only
The honky-tonk green of the road from the plains to the beach
Cars pitched up for an evening of reckless beauty each
Out late for what they can get lonely
But happy to be here with the buildings behind them shops
And houses here where a dim-lit world becomes lepidolite
Tarpaulins play across tables and put-me-ups lifting
A bird walks to the edge of the water stops
Briefly pink like an aeroplane hurled against twilight
Moving forward *in excelsis* drifting

ENDS

A Poem by Walter de la Mare

Go, songs, to the heart of government,
Quarrel directly with thin-lipped bureaucrats,
Dispense advice to the shiftlessly fat
For all things being equal they shall inherit the earth.

Turn up places, regional shopping centres for example,
Announce the death of all description
[Some description is good –
                              'In Maidstone, Winter!'
The subject of animals, on the other hand, is closed.]

Go, to those who live in small towns,
To those whose parents lived in small towns,
Dwell with them for they too are curious,
Show them wit and a smart pair of heels.

Go to the decision-makers.
                    [For they made no decision.]
Go to the weary and the down-at-heart,
Kiss them, tell them they will not be audited.
Go to the stolid.
                    Poke them.

Go to Guildford,
Go to the deadened by work,
Go to those incapacitated by middle age.
Go to lunch,
Speak freely with those around you
Of the pleasures of omelette, a light spirit;
Against the tyranny of seriousness,
Against the tyranny of the career,
Invite a conversation on the subject of apathy.
Animate,
Make large and frankly unmistakable gestures.
Denounce subtlety
Insist on subtlety.

Excite.
Speak with a sudden clarity.
Fall over upon exiting a moving bus.

In Autumn, shake out the seeds from any remaining bedding plants.
Fall over.
Dust yourself off.

Two Figures

Figure 1

Practical Material Determining Grounds
in the principle of morality
are

Subjective

External	*Internal*
Of education	Of physical feeling
(according to Montaigne)	(according to Epicurus)
Of the civil constitution	Of moral feeling
(according to Mandeville)	(according to Hutcheson)

Objective

Internal	*External*
Of perfection	Of the will of God
(according to Wolff	(according to Crusius and
and the Stoics)	other theological moralists)

Figure 2

TABLE
of the categories of freedom with respect to the concepts of the good and evil

1
Of quantity
Subjective, in accordance with maxims (*intentions of the will* of the individual)
Objective, in accordance with principles (*precepts*)
A priori objective as well as subjective principles of freedom (*laws*)

2	3
Of quality	Of relation
Practical rules of *commission*	To *personality*
(*praeceptivae*)	To the *condition* of the person
Practical rules of *omission*	*Reciprocally*, of one person
(*prohibitivae*)	to the condition of others
Practical rules *exceptions*	
(*exceptivae*)	

4
Of modality
The *permitted* and the *forbidden*
Duty and what is *contrary to duty*
Perfect and *imperfect* duty

To a Friend

Only last night I was reading Kant again.
This morning
                    I finished a poem.
I drink coffee.
I eat when I need to.

I send you my love.

David.

A Note on the Title

For those unfamiliar with the workings of British public life at the end of the twentieth and the beginning of the twenty-first century, Peter Mandelson was a politician. An aesthete by temperament, and sometime Director of Communications, his most enduring contribution was symbolic, changing the emblem of his party from a flag to a rose; a rose; a rose;
a rose.

This is not his house: